Beginners Guide To Financial Independence And Early Retirement (FIRE)

Table of Contents

1. Understanding FIRE

(1) - 1.1 What is FIRE?

(2) - 1.2 The History of FIRE Movement

(3) - 1.3 Key Principles of Financial Independence

2. Setting Your Financial Goals

(1) - 2.1 Short-term vs Long-term Goals

(2) - 2.2 SMART Goal Framework

(3) - 2.3 Prioritizing Financial Milestones

3. Budgeting Basics

(1) - 3.1 Types of Budgeting Methods

(2) - 3.2 Creating a Personal Budget

(3) - 3.3 Budgeting for Variable Expenses

4. Tracking Income and Expenses

(1) - 4.1 Tools for Tracking Finances

(2) - 4.2 Categorizing Your Expenses

(3) - 4.3 Reviewing and Adjusting Your Budget

5. The Importance of Emergency Funds

(1) - 5.1 How Much to Save?

(2) - 5.2 Where to Keep Your Emergency Fund

(3) - 5.3 Building Your Emergency Fund Strategy

6. Debt Management

(1) - 6.1 Types of Debt

(2) - 6.2 Strategies for Paying Off Debt

(3) - 6.3 Avoiding Debt in the Future

7. Investing Fundamentals

(1) - 7.1 Types of Investment Vehicles

(2) - 7.2 Understanding Risk Tolerance

(3) - 7.3 Building a Diversified Portfolio

8. Retirement Accounts Explored

(1) - 8.1 Types of Retirement Accounts

(2) - 8.2 Tax Advantages of Retirement Accounts

(3) - 8.3 Strategies for Maximizing Contributions

9. Passive Income Streams

(1) - 9.1 What is Passive Income?

(2) - 9.2 Different Types of Passive Income

(3) - 9.3 Building Your Passive Income Portfolio

10. The Role of Insurance

(1) - 10.1 Insurance Types You Need

(2) - 10.2 Evaluating Your Insurance Needs

(3) - 10.3 Minimizing Your Insurance Costs

11. Tax Planning for FIRE

(1) - 11.1 Understanding Your Tax Bracket

(2) - 11.2 Tax-efficient Investment Strategies

(3) - 11.3 Deductions and Credits to Consider

12. Lifestyle Design

(1) - 12.1 Aligning Lifestyle with Values

(2) - 12.2 Minimalism and Its Financial Benefits

(3) - 12.3 Creating a Vision Board for Your Future

13. Overcoming Psychological Barriers

(1) - 13.1 The Emotional Impact of Money

(2) - 13.2 Cultivating a Wealth Mindset

(3) - 13.3 Staying Motivated on Your FIRE Journey

14. Creating a Support System

(1) - 14.1 Building a Community of Like-minded Individuals

(2) - 14.2 Utilizing Online Resources

(3) - 14.3 Finding a Financial Mentor

15. Transitioning to Early Retirement

(1) - 15.1 Preparing for the Shift

(2) - 15.2 Managing Your Time After Retirement

(3) - 15.3 Staying Financially Fit in Retirement

1. Understanding FIRE

1.1 What is FIRE?

The concept of Financial Independence, Retire Early (FIRE) is an empowering movement aimed at achieving the freedom to choose how you spend your time without being tethered to a traditional job. It attracts a diverse range of people who seek to break free from the typical 9-to-5 grind. The appeal lies in the idea that by diligently saving, investing, and cutting unnecessary expenses, individuals can accumulate enough wealth to sustain their desired lifestyle well before reaching the conventional retirement age. Many adherents of the FIRE movement dream of traveling the world, pursuing passion projects, or simply enjoying more time with family and friends without the stress of financial constraints.

Understanding the FIRE movement requires familiarization with key terms that frame the journey toward financial independence. For starters, 'financial independence' refers to having sufficient income from investments, savings, or other passive sources to cover your expenses without needing earned income from a job. 'Retire early' does not necessarily mean stopping all work; rather, it emphasizes the freedom to choose when and how you want to work. Another essential term is 'lean FIRE,' which describes a more frugal lifestyle aiming for a lower cost of living, whereas 'fat FIRE' suggests a more comfortable living while still achieving early retirement. Other relevant terms include 'withdrawal rate,' which is the percentage of your total savings that you can sustainably withdraw each year in retirement without running out of money, and 'side hustle,' referring to any work you do outside of your primary job to boost income, which is often a key component of the FIRE strategy.

Engaging with the FIRE movement opens up a wealth of strategies that can enhance financial literacy and budgeting techniques. One practical tip for those interested in pursuing FIRE is to start tracking your expenses meticulously. This involves knowing exactly where your money goes each month and identifying areas where you can cut back. By gaining visibility into your spending habits, you can make informed decisions on how to save more effectively and allocate funds toward investment opportunities. This habit lays the groundwork for not only achieving financial independence but also gaining confidence in personal finance management.

1.2 The History of FIRE Movement

The origins of the FIRE movement can be traced back to the 1990s, a time when personal finance literature began to gain popularity. This period saw the publication of key works such as Your Money or Your Life by Vicki Robin and Joe Dominguez, which laid the groundwork for many principles central to the FIRE philosophy. The authors emphasized the importance of tracking expenses, living frugally, and understanding the relationship between money and happiness. Their model encouraged individuals to critically assess their spending habits and prioritize saving to achieve financial freedom. The concept of reducing one's expenses drastically and saving a significant portion of income was a radical shift from traditional notions of financial security, which typically hinged on long-term employment and steady income through the years.

As the FIRE movement gained momentum, it began to evolve and diversify through the 2000s and beyond. More people started to adopt the principles of aggressive saving and investing, spurred on by the rise of the internet and financial blogs. The advent of online communities allowed individuals to share their experiences, strategies, and successes. This digital connectivity fostered a broader understanding of investment strategies, including index fund investing and real estate, further elevating the movement. In this new environment, the narrative shifted from merely pursuing early retirement to achieving various lifestyle choices that align with personal values, such as travel, creative pursuits, or volunteer work. The flexibility of the FIRE movement became appealing to those who sought more meaningful lives beyond the constraints of conventional employment.

The FIRE movement continues to captivate a diverse audience, embracing those who wish to retire early as well as those simply aiming to gain more control over their financial futures. With various subcategories like Fat FIRE, Lean FIRE, and Barista FIRE, the community has developed a range of strategies to suit different lifestyles and financial goals. This evolution highlights a growing realization that financial independence is not a one-size-fits-all model. Instead, it is a customizable journey shaped by individual circumstances and aspirations. Whether it's through aggressive saving, smart investing, or simply cutting unnecessary expenses, the FIRE movement remains a powerful philosophy for helping individuals seek financial autonomy and the freedom to pursue their passions. Practicing intentional budgeting, whether through the use of apps or traditional methods, can streamline this journey, making it easier to visualize goals and track progress along the way.

1.3 Key Principles of Financial Independence

Core tenets of the Financial Independence, Retire Early (FIRE) philosophy revolve around careful financial planning, mindful spending, and intentional saving. At its heart, the pursuit of financial independence is about having control over your time and choices, rather than being chained to a nine-to-five job solely for the sake of income. A critical concept here is the importance of understanding your financial situation. This includes being aware of your net worth, income sources, and expenses. Knowing where your money is going helps you make informed decisions that can significantly accelerate your journey toward independence. Additionally, embracing frugality does not mean depriving yourself; it's about prioritizing what truly matters to you and eliminating unnecessary expenses that do not bring value to your life. This philosophy emphasizes that small, consistent actions often lead to substantial long-term results.

Lifestyle choices play a pivotal role in achieving financial independence. Adjusting how you live can directly impact your ability to save and invest. For instance, minimizing housing expenses by choosing a more affordable living situation can free up a significant portion of your income for saving. Embracing a minimalist lifestyle leads to fewer material burdens and often enhances well-being, allowing individuals to focus on experiences rather than possessions. Transportation choices also matter; using public transport, biking, or walking can substantially reduce monthly expenses. Opting for home-cooked meals over dining out often reflects a significant financial saving. These lifestyle adjustments might require some initial effort, but they cultivate habits that support long-term financial goals. Living below your means and prioritizing savings over consumption not only improves your financial situation but also fosters a mindset that aligns with financial independence.

Establishing a budget is an essential practical step that can contribute significantly to your journey toward financial independence. A robust budget helps keep spending in check, ensuring you allocate sufficient funds to savings and investments while also enjoying life. Track your expenses to identify areas where you can cut back and increase your savings rate. As you gain more experience in managing your finances and refining your budget, you will discover what strategies work best for you—whether it's automating your savings, exploring side hustles for additional income, or setting specific financial goals that guide your decision-making. Developing these strategies and maintaining a strong focus on your financial objectives is key to building the foundations of your independent lifestyle.

2. Setting Your Financial Goals

2.1 Short-term vs Long-term Goals

Understanding the difference between short-term and long-term financial objectives is crucial for anyone looking to achieve financial independence or early retirement. Short-term goals typically focus on achievable milestones within a year or less. These might include saving for a vacation, paying off credit card debt, or emergency savings. In contrast, long-term goals stretch beyond a year and often involve significant financial targets like retirement savings, purchasing a home, or funding children's education. Recognizing these categories helps you prioritize your efforts and allocate resources effectively, steering your financial decisions toward what truly matters to you.

The time horizon you set for your goals fundamentally influences your planning approach. Short-term goals usually require looking at your immediate cash flow, allowing for quick adjustments and involving less risk. They can be managed through straightforward budgeting techniques, such as the envelope system or regular savings contributions. Long-term goals demand a different mindset, often necessitating investments that can withstand market fluctuations and compounding interest over time. These goals require a broader perspective, not just on how your money is allocated today, but how it will grow and change over the years. Being mindful of the time frame allows for a more strategic approach to saving and investing, making sure your financial plans align with your life objectives.

In practice, balancing short-term and long-term goals can provide a roadmap to financial success. Prioritizing short-term objectives creates a sense of achievement and helps build the financial discipline necessary for tackling larger goals. Meanwhile, keeping an eye on long-term aspirations ensures that you remain focused on your ultimate financial independence. A useful tip is to regularly evaluate and adjust your goals based on life changes; as your circumstances evolve, so should your financial objectives. Creating a flexible plan allows for adaptation, ensuring that both your short-term needs and long-term dreams work in harmony.

2.2 SMART Goal Framework

Specificity is essential when setting goals, especially in the realm of personal finance and budgeting. A specific goal clearly defines what you want to achieve, eliminating vague aspirations that can lead to confusion or lack of direction. Instead of saying, I want to save money, a specific goal would be, I want to save $10,000 for a down payment on a house by the end of next year. This clarity allows you to focus your efforts and makes it easier to create a plan. To enhance specificity, consider details such as what steps you will take to reach your goal, the exact amount you are targeting, and a concrete timeline for completion. These details help transform your goal into actionable items, paving the way for better financial management and progress towards financial independence.

Measurability is another crucial aspect of the SMART goal framework. Establishing criteria for measuring your progress towards your goals helps you to stay on track and motivated. When a goal is measurable, you can see how far you've come and how much further you need to go. For instance, instead of just aiming to get better at budgeting, you might set a goal of reviewing my budget every month and adjusting my spending to save an additional $200 each month. This way, you can track your savings and monitor your budgeting efficiency over time. Using tools like spreadsheets or budgeting apps can help keep your measurements clear and organized, making it easier to celebrate small wins along the way and adjust your strategies as necessary.

By combining specificity with measurability, you create a solid foundation for your financial goals. As you embark on your journey towards financial independence and early retirement, remember that every successful plan starts with clear, actionable steps that you can measure. A useful tip is to regularly revisit and revise your goals to ensure they remain relevant and challenging. This dynamic approach allows you to adapt your strategies as your financial situation changes, ensuring continued progress toward your FIRE aspirations.

2.3 Prioritizing Financial Milestones

Understanding your financial journey requires recognizing the key milestones that mark significant achievements along the way. These milestones act as markers that help you gauge your progress and adjust your strategies as needed. Start with establishing an emergency fund, which serves as your safety net during uncertain times. Aim for savings that cover three to six months of living expenses to provide financial stability. Next, consider paying off high-interest debt, as reducing this burden can free up significant cash flow. Whether it's credit card debt or a personal loan, eliminating these costs early will enhance your overall financial health.

Another critical milestone is the accumulation of retirement savings. Setting up a retirement account, such as an IRA or a 401(k), and contributing regularly can set the foundation for future financial independence. As you progress, it's crucial to focus on building net worth through investments, whether in stocks, real estate, or other assets. Not only should you aim for growth, but it's also important to continually reassess your portfolio to ensure it aligns with your evolving goals.

Prioritizing your financial milestones helps you focus your efforts and makes your journey less overwhelming. Start by analyzing your personal circumstances. Are you in significant debt, or do you have savings that you want to invest? Your current financial situation plays a pivotal role in determining what comes first. It may be wise to prioritize paying off high-interest debts before moving on to saving for retirement. Consider your short-term needs versus your long-term goals; this balance is essential for effective prioritization.

A well-structured technique for prioritizing is the SMART criteria, which stands for Specific, Measurable, Achievable, Relevant, and Time-bound. Each milestone you set should meet these criteria, ensuring you have clear objectives that are realistic given your current financial standing. Additionally, embracing flexibility in your plan is crucial. As your circumstances change — whether due to a raise, a job change, or personal life events — revisit your priorities to stay in alignment with your goals. A practical tip is to review your financial milestones regularly, ideally every few months, to ensure you're on the right track and making necessary adjustments.

3. Budgeting Basics

3.1 *Types of Budgeting Methods*

Budgeting is essential for managing your finances effectively, especially when you're on a journey toward financial independence and early retirement. Among the popular methods, zero-based budgeting stands out as a practical technique where every dollar is assigned a specific role, ensuring that your income minus your expenses equals zero. This method encourages you to scrutinize where every penny goes, helping eliminate unnecessary spending. The envelope system relies on physical cash divided into labeled envelopes for different spending categories, making it easier to adhere to your budget without overspending. Lastly, the 50/30/20 rule simplifies budgeting into three main categories: 50% of your income goes towards needs, 30% towards wants, and 20% towards savings and debt repayment, creating a balanced approach to managing your money.

Selecting the right budgeting approach for your individual circumstances involves weighing several factors. First, consider your financial goals and lifestyle. If you're looking to be strict and detailed about every dollar, zero-based budgeting might work best for you. If you prefer a simpler, intuitive method, the 50/30/20 rule could be more appealing. Additionally, assess your spending habits. The envelope system may be particularly effective if you find yourself frequently exceeding budgeted amounts. Lastly, think about the time you can commit to budgeting. Some methods require regular reviews and adjustments, while others are more set-and-forget. Understanding your own financial behavior and lifestyle preferences can lead you to the budgeting method that fits best, helping to maintain motivation and build better financial habits.

Implementing an effective budgeting method can significantly enhance your financial management, putting you one step closer to achieving your goals. Whichever method you choose, ensure that it feels comfortable and sustainable, allowing you to manage your finances while still enjoying life. A practical tip is to start with what feels most manageable to you; even small changes can lead to significant improvements in your budgeting effectiveness over time.

3.2 Creating a Personal Budget

Creating your first budget can feel like a daunting task, but taking it step by step can transform this experience into an empowering journey towards financial stability. Start by gathering all your financial documents, including your pay stubs, bank statements, and bills. With these in hand, you can get a clear picture of your income and expenses. Begin by listing your total income, which includes your salary, bonuses, or any side hustles. It's essential to be honest and realistic about what you actually earn, as this forms the foundation of your budgeting. Next, make a detailed list of your expenses. Divide them into fixed expenses, like rent or mortgage, and variable expenses, such as groceries and entertainment. This distinction helps you identify areas where you might cut back. Calculate your net income by subtracting your total expenses from your total income. If you find yourself in a deficit, it's a signal to adjust your spending habits accordingly. Finally, allocate a portion of your budget to savings and investments. This step is crucial for those pursuing financial independence, as it builds the foundation necessary for achieving your long-term goals.

Customizing your budget is where the real magic happens. Remember, there is no one-size-fits-all solution. Your financial situation is unique, shaped by your spending habits, lifestyle, and goals. Consider using budgeting tools or apps that allow for flexibility and adjustments as needed. Set specific financial goals, whether it's saving for a vacation, a new car, or even your retirement. By categorizing your spending to reflect these goals, you can prioritize what matters most to you. Another effective strategy is the 50/30/20 rule, where 50% of your income goes to needs, 30% to wants, and 20% to savings or debt repayment. However, feel free to tweak this model based on your personal circumstances. If travel is a priority for you, perhaps you allocate more than 30% to wants, adjusting other categories accordingly. Regularly revisiting and adjusting your budget ensures that it remains aligned with your financial journey and evolving priorities. Remember, budgeting is not about deprivation; it's about creating freedom with your finances.

As you embark on this budgeting adventure, consider setting aside a small "fun fund" within your budget to allow for occasional indulgences without guilt. This approach not only keeps you motivated but also encourages you to stick to your financial goals over the long haul. Establishing a solid budget is the first step towards taking control of your finances and paving the way toward financial independence.

3.3 Budgeting for Variable Expenses

Identifying variable expenses is crucial for effective budgeting. Variable expenses are those costs that fluctuate from month to month, unlike fixed expenses which remain constant. Examples of variable expenses include groceries, dining out, entertainment, and unexpected medical bills. Recognizing these differences allows you to prepare for and respond to changes in your financial landscape. This understanding can set the foundation for better financial planning, enabling you to allocate your resources more thoughtfully. You might find it beneficial to track these variable expenses closely for several months. By monitoring how these amounts shift, you can form a clearer picture of your spending patterns and prepare better for the future.

Strategies for flexibility will help you manage your finances when confronted with unpredictable variable expenses. One effective approach is to create a variable expense fund. This fund acts as a buffer, providing a cushion for those months when your spending spikes unexpectedly. Allocate a specific amount of money each month towards this fund, and when a month sees higher expenditures, you can draw from it without derailing your overall budget. Another technique involves prioritizing these variable expenses. When you face fluctuations, be mindful of what is essential versus what can be adjusted or reduced. This critical evaluation empowers you to stay on course with your financial goals while accommodating necessary spending.

Ultimately, embracing flexibility and fostering mindful spending habits can lead to a more stable financial situation. Consider utilizing budgeting apps that can aid in tracking both fixed and variable expenses, enabling a comprehensive view of your finances. These tools can simplify the process and help you make informed decisions on the fly. One practical tip to enhance your budgeting for variable expenses is to plan for variability itself. Instead of worrying about every dollar, anticipate some fluctuations by budgeting for 10-20% more in categories you know vary. This buffer will help you handle life's financial surprises without stress.

4. Tracking Income and Expenses

4.1 Tools for Tracking Finances

In today's digital age, various apps and software can make managing finances more accessible and efficient than ever before. Many of these digital solutions offer features that allow users to track spending, create budgets, and even set financial goals. Popular apps like Mint, YNAB (You Need A Budget), and PocketGuard provide intuitive interfaces that give you a clear picture of your financial situation at a glance. With these tools, users can connect their bank accounts, analyze spending trends, and receive alerts when they approach budget limits. Furthermore, many of these platforms also provide educational resources, helping users understand nothing more than what they spend, but why they spend it. By incorporating visual graphs and summaries, they help in making financial information less daunting and more actionable. Digital tools can significantly streamline the budgeting process, which is a key part of achieving financial independence and making informed decisions toward early retirement.

On the other hand, traditional methods for tracking finances, like spreadsheets and pen-and-paper techniques, still hold value, especially for those who prefer a more hands-on approach. Spreadsheets, such as Excel or Google Sheets, offer the flexibility to customize tracking according to personal financial situations. Users can create their own formulas to calculate expenses, income, and savings goals, allowing for deeper insights into their finances. Writing down expenditures may seem outdated, but there is power in physical writing; it can enhance memory retention and provide a sense of accountability. Moreover, the act of reviewing receipts or budgeting categories manually can foster a better understanding of financial habits and encourage mindful spending. This combination of digital and manual tracking techniques can cater to different preferences, giving users a comprehensive view of their financial health.

Utilizing these tracking tools is not just about maintaining a budget; it's about building a mindset of financial awareness that aligns with the principles of financial independence and early retirement. Consider setting aside a specific time each week to review your financial situation using both digital and manual methods. This consistent practice reinforces your commitment to understanding and improving your financial circumstances, enhancing your journey towards achieving your financial goals.

4.2 Categorizing Your Expenses

Identifying and organizing your expenses into meaningful categories is vital for effective personal finance management. When you categorize your expenses, you start to see where your money really goes. Common categories include fixed expenses, such as rent or mortgage, and variable expenses, including groceries and entertainment. You can also create more specific categories like transportation or personal care. By doing this, you gain insight into spending patterns and can pinpoint areas where you might cut back. For example, if you notice you are spending significantly on dining out, you can decide to allocate some of that money toward savings or investments. Tailoring your categories to reflect your lifestyle and financial goals makes tracking progress easier and helps maintain focus on your objectives.

Understanding the value of categorization can revolutionize your budgeting decisions. By seeing your expenses categorized visually, it becomes simpler to identify unnecessary expenditures and prioritize where to allocate funds. It can highlight areas where you may spend impulsively or excessively. This practice also fosters accountability; when you know your categories and limits, you become more conscious of your financial choices. A well-organized budget can pave the way for building savings, investing wisely, or even pursuing financial independence and early retirement. Categorization serves not just as a framework for understanding spending, but also as a proactive tool for shaping your financial future.

To maximize the benefits of expense categorization, consider regularly reviewing your spending habits. This could be monthly or quarterly, depending on what works for you. This practice allows you to adjust your categories as needed, ensuring they remain relevant to your goals. Keep in mind, flexibility is essential in budgeting. What works today might not align with your priorities tomorrow. Stay diligent and use your categorized expenses to guide your financial journey in a way that brings you closer to your FIRE aspirations.

4.3 Reviewing and Adjusting Your Budget

Regularly assessing your financial plan is essential for staying on track towards your goals. A budget is not a static document; instead, it should evolve alongside your life circumstances and financial situation. By setting aside time each month to review your budget, you can identify areas where you may have overspent or where you can save even more. This regular examination helps you stay connected with your financial habits and can often highlight patterns that might otherwise go unnoticed. Addressing these patterns before they lead to serious overspending is crucial for maintaining control over your finances.

Making adjustments to your budget when life changes is key to achieving financial independence. Transitioning jobs, relocating, or undergoing major life events such as marriage or having a child can all impact your budget significantly. It's important to revisit your spending and saving priorities in light of these changes. Try separating your essential expenses from discretionary spending to see where flexibility lies. This approach can help you reallocate funds efficiently, accommodating new needs without derailing your main financial goals. Keeping open communication with your partner or family about budgeting changes can also foster a sense of teamwork and financial alignment.

One practical technique to facilitate this process is to set up a biannual or annual financial review. During these reviews, consider all aspects of your financial life including investments, debt repayment, and emergency savings. Ask yourself if your financial goals are still relevant and whether your budget aligns with those goals. This proactive approach not only enhances your financial management but also empowers you to make informed decisions. Remember, the journey toward financial independence and early retirement is not just about how much you save but how adaptable and engaged you are with your financial narrative.

5. The Importance of Emergency Funds

5.1 How Much to Save?

Determining the right amount to save for an emergency fund is crucial and varies widely based on personal circumstances. A common guideline suggests setting aside three to six months' worth of living expenses. However, your unique situation might necessitate a different approach. Consider factors such as your employment stability, whether you have dependents, and any additional financial obligations. For instance, if you work in a field where job security is less stable, or if you have dependents who rely on your income, aiming for a larger cushion can provide peace of mind. Furthermore, think about your expenses: identify essential costs like housing, food, transportation, and healthcare. Once you have a clear picture of your baseline requirements, you can set a goal that aligns with your lifestyle and risk tolerance. Adjusting this amount over time as your life circumstances shift is also important, ensuring your emergency fund grows with you.

A robust emergency fund is not just a safety net; it contributes significantly to your overall financial stability. Having a solid amount saved reduces stress during unexpected events, allowing you to navigate life's uncertainties with greater confidence. This fund serves as a buffer against the unexpected costs of car repairs, medical emergencies, or job loss, which can derail financial plans if you are unprepared. By prioritizing an emergency fund, you provide yourself with financial freedom, enabling you to pursue opportunities without the fear of financial repercussions. Moreover, it allows you to avoid high-interest debt that often accompanies emergencies, keeping you on track to achieve your financial independence and early retirement goals. Focusing on consistently building your emergency fund provides not only immediate security but also serves as a foundation for long-term financial health, contributing to your journey towards FIRE.

To effectively enhance your emergency fund, consider automating your savings. By setting up a regular transfer from your checking to your savings account, you ensure that saving becomes a habit rather than an afterthought. Start with a manageable amount that won't disrupt your budget, and gradually increase this transfer as your financial situation improves. This approach not only simplifies the process but also keeps your savings growing without the temptation to spend. Remember, every bit counts, and small, consistent contributions can lead to a substantial fund over time.

5.2 Where to Keep Your Emergency Fund

Choosing the best account types for your emergency fund is essential to ensure your savings are safe and readily available. High-yield savings accounts often stand out as a favorable option. These accounts typically offer better interest rates than standard savings accounts, which means your money can grow more while still being accessible. Additionally, many online banks provide these high-yield accounts with low fees or no fees at all, contributing to your overall savings strategy. Some credit unions also offer competitive rates, making them a viable alternative. However, it's crucial to consider your bank's access policies and the ease of transferring funds when you need them. Other options include money market accounts, which can sometimes offer similar benefits but may come with higher minimum balance requirements. Ultimately, the ideal account for your emergency fund balances the dual priorities of growth through interest and quick access when you need cash in a pinch.

Access and growth are two pivotal factors when deciding where to keep your emergency fund. You want to ensure your money is easy to get to in case of unexpected expenses, like a medical emergency or sudden home repairs. A solid emergency fund should guarantee you access to your cash without delays or excessive penalties. While a basic savings account provides quick access, it often lacks significant interest-earning potential. In contrast, high-yield savings accounts or money market accounts can provide higher returns, but it's essential to check their withdrawal limitations and fees. Some accounts may limit the number of withdrawals you can make each month, so understanding these terms is vital. Striking a balance between easy access and potential growth from interest will serve you well in maintaining your financial safety net.

When deciding where to park your emergency fund, remember to consider your financial goals and personal habits. The right account can make a significant difference in how effectively you manage your finances. Assess your spending patterns and the likelihood of needing quick access to your money. Sometimes, having a portion of your emergency fund in a more accessible account and another portion in a high-yield option can be a smart strategy. This way, you are prepared for immediate needs while still gaining some interest. Additionally, regularly revisiting your choices can ensure they still meet your needs as your financial situation changes over time. Keeping an emergency fund isn't just about where you place your money; it's about having a strategy that works best for you and empowers your journey toward financial independence.

5.3 Building Your Emergency Fund Strategy

Creating a solid plan to build your emergency fund is essential for achieving financial independence. Begin by determining how much money you need to feel secure during unexpected events, such as medical emergencies, job loss, or major repairs. A common guideline is to aim for three to six months' worth of living expenses. However, depending on your personal situation, you may need more. Next, analyze your current financial situation, including your income, expenses, and any debts. This assessment will help you understand how much you can realistically set aside each month. Consider breaking your savings goal into smaller, manageable milestones, which can make the process feel less daunting and more achievable. Automating your savings is another great strategy. Set up a separate savings account dedicated to your emergency fund, and arrange for a certain amount of money to be transferred from your checking account to this savings account each payday. This way, saving becomes a habit rather than an afterthought.

Reviewing and adjusting your emergency fund strategy periodically is crucial for ensuring it meets your evolving needs. As your life circumstances change—like a new job, marriage, or children—so too might your financial obligations and risks. Ideally, you should reassess your emergency fund at least once a year or after a major life change. Take stock of your current expenses and the stability of your income sources. If you've recently received a promotion or a raise, consider increasing your savings goal, or if your living expenses have decreased, you might find that you can reduce the target amount you need. Additionally, stay informed about the cost of living in your area and other economic factors that can impact your financial security. Recognizing these shifts allows you to make smart adjustments to ensure your emergency fund is always sufficient.

To keep your emergency fund effective, remember that not all savings are created equal. Keep your emergency money fluid and accessible, but try to earn interest by placing it in a high-yield savings account. This way, you're not only protecting your finances against sudden events but also allowing your money to grow slightly while you save for a rainy day. Regularly reviewing your emergency fund strategy alongside your overall budget can lead to a more comprehensive understanding of your financial landscape. Incremental adjustments can have a significant impact, helping you achieve financial independence more effectively and ensuring peace of mind as you navigate life's uncertainties.

6. Debt Management

6.1 *Types of Debt*

Understanding debt is crucial for anyone seeking financial independence, especially those attracted to the FIRE movement. There are two primary types of debt: secured and unsecured. Secured debt is backed by collateral, such as a house or a car. If you fail to repay secured debts, the lender can take the asset as compensation. This type of debt often comes with lower interest rates because the lender has a safety net. On the other hand, unsecured debt does not require collateral, meaning it is riskier for lenders. Examples include credit card debt and personal loans. Unsecured debt typically carries higher interest rates due to the greater risk posed to lenders. Knowing the difference between these two types helps you make informed decisions and manage potential risks, impacting your personal finance strategy significantly.

Interest rates play a pivotal role in how different types of debt affect your finances. For secured loans, the interest rates are generally lower, making them more manageable over the long term. This feature is particularly beneficial when financing major purchases, as it allows you to spread payments over several years without overwhelming interest costs. In contrast, unsecured debt usually comes with high-interest rates, which can lead to a steep financial burden if not managed carefully. When you carry a large balance on credit cards, for example, even small interest rate increases can lead to significant costs. Understanding how interest rates work can empower you to choose the right debt products and strategies. Paying attention to these rates is essential, as they can dictate your budgeting and overall financial strategy.

Utilizing this knowledge effectively can significantly improve your path toward financial independence. One practical tip is to prioritize paying off high-interest unsecured debt first while maintaining timely payments on secured debt. This strategy not only reduces the amount paid in interest over time but also establishes a solid foundation for your financial health. By managing your debts wisely, you can allocate more resources to savings and investment, bringing you closer to your early retirement goals.

6.2 Strategies for Paying Off Debt

The debt snowball and debt avalanche methods are two well-known strategies for paying off debt, each with its unique approach and benefits. The debt snowball method emphasizes emotional motivation by focusing on the smallest debts first. You list your debts from smallest to largest and pay as much as possible on the smallest debt while making minimum payments on the others. Once the smallest debt is cleared, you move on to the next smallest, using the payment you were making on the first debt to tackle the next one. This method can provide quick wins, boosting your confidence and motivation as you see debts eliminated little by little.

On the other hand, the debt avalanche method is more mathematically driven. This strategy directs your payments toward the highest-interest debt first, regardless of its size. The rationale here is rooted in the long-term savings on interest payments, as paying off high-interest debt sooner means you'll pay less overall. While it typically results in a faster reduction of debt and less money spent on interest, it may take longer to see debts disappearing, which can be less motivating for some individuals. Understanding these two approaches can help you find the right fit for your personality and financial situation.

Crafting a solid payment plan is crucial for successfully managing and eliminating debt. The first step involves gathering a clear view of your financial situation by compiling a list of all your debts, including the total amount owed, minimum monthly payments, and interest rates. With this information in hand, you can choose between the snowball method or the avalanche method based on what resonates with your goals and feelings. After making your choice, outline a budget that allocates a specific amount each month toward debt repayment along with your essential living expenses.

Regularly reviewing and adjusting your plan is another essential component. It's important to track your progress and celebrate small victories along the way to maintain motivation. Consider setting up automatic payments to ensure you never miss a due date and always pay at least the minimum required amount. If you experience fluctuations in income or unexpected expenses, stay flexible and revisit your budget to allocate any additional funds toward your debt when possible. This proactive approach not only enhances your chance of success in paying off debts but also fosters a sense of control over your finances, which is crucial for those pursuing financial independence and early retirement.

Remember, every little bit helps when it comes to debt reduction. Try to find a way to funnel any extra money — whether it's from a side hustle, a gift, or cutting discretionary spending — into your debt payments. This can make a significant impact over time and help bring you closer to your goal of financial freedom.

6.3 Avoiding Debt in the Future

Establishing strong financial habits is essential for avoiding debt in the future. Begin by creating and sticking to a realistic budget that outlines your income, expenses, and savings goals. Track your spending meticulously; this awareness helps you identify unnecessary expenditures and prioritize your financial goals. It's beneficial to set aside an emergency fund that covers three to six months of living expenses, creating a safety net that reduces the need for credit when unexpected costs arise.

Living within your means is crucial. This means resisting the urge to keep up with the lifestyle of others and instead focusing on what you truly need. When making a purchase, ask yourself if it aligns with your financial goals or if it's merely a fleeting desire. Planning and saving for larger purchases can help you avoid relying on credit. Utilizing cash or debit cards instead of credit cards can further decrease the likelihood of falling into debt. These simple behavioral changes foster a healthier relationship with money and fortify your commitment to financial independence.

Financial education is a powerful tool in the quest for financial independence and debt avoidance. Understanding key concepts, such as interest rates, credit scores, and the consequences of debt, arms you with the knowledge to make informed choices. Seek out resources like books, online courses, and podcasts that cover personal finance topics. Knowledge about managing debts, setting up automatic savings, and investing can drastically alter your financial trajectory, helping you steer clear of pitfalls that could lead to reaccumulating debt.

Engaging in discussions about finance, whether with friends, family, or in community groups, can also enhance your understanding. Sharing experiences and learning from others often sheds light on practical solutions and innovative budgeting strategies. Additionally, consider tracking your credit report regularly. Awareness of your credit standing allows you to address any issues before they escalate. By committing to continuous learning about finances, you empower yourself to navigate money matters wisely, further supporting your journey toward financial independence.

Utilizing apps and tools designed for personal finance can aid in budgeting and managing expenses effectively. Setting financial goals accompanied by timelines helps keep your motivation high while also clarifying your priorities. Being proactive in your financial education and habits not only helps avoid debt but also lays a solid foundation for a future of financial freedom.

7. Investing Fundamentals

7.1 Types of Investment Vehicles

Investment options abound, each offering distinct opportunities and challenges. Stocks represent ownership in individual companies. When you buy a stock, you acquire a piece of that company, which can grow in value or pay dividends based on its performance. On the other hand, bonds are a form of debt. When you purchase a bond, you're essentially lending money to a government or corporation in exchange for periodic interest payments and the return of the bond's face value at maturity. Then there are exchange-traded funds (ETFs), which combine elements of both stocks and bonds. An ETF holds a collection of assets, allowing investors to buy a slice of a diverse portfolio without having to select each individual investment. Lastly, real estate provides a tangible asset that can generate rental income and appreciate over time, making it a popular choice for those looking to build wealth outside of traditional financial markets.

Understanding the trade-offs associated with these investment vehicles is crucial for making informed decisions. Most investment types come with varying levels of risk, return, and liquidity. Stocks can offer high returns, especially over the long term, but they also carry significant risk due to market volatility. Bonds, while generally considered safer than stocks, may yield lower returns, especially in low-interest-rate environments. ETFs offer diversification, which can reduce risk, but they still carry some equity risk depending on their holdings. Real estate can provide steady cash flow and asset appreciation, yet it requires significant upfront capital and can be less liquid due to the time it takes to buy or sell properties.

When considering where to place your money, it's essential to evaluate your risk tolerance, investment goals, and the impact of liquidity on your financial situation. For those pursuing Financial Independence and Early Retirement, balance is key. A well-thought-out mix of assets can provide both growth potential and stability. Continuous education about these vehicles and regular portfolio review can help you adapt to market changes and stay aligned with your financial objectives. Keep in mind that the best investment vehicle for you is the one that fits your circumstances and goals, enabling you to make confident financial decisions.

7.2 Understanding Risk Tolerance

Understanding your risk tolerance is a fundamental step in your journey toward financial independence and early retirement. Risk tolerance is not merely about your financial situation; it also incorporates your personality, life stage, and financial goals. To assess your risk, start by using online risk assessment questionnaires. Many financial websites offer simple quizzes that can help gauge how much risk you are comfortable taking with your investments. These tools typically ask about your investment goals, time horizon, and how you would react to market fluctuations. By reflecting on the potential emotional responses to losses or gains, you can pinpoint a clearer picture of your risk tolerance.

Another useful method involves analyzing your past investment behaviors. Look back at your experiences with investing and consider how you felt during market downturns. Did you panic and sell off your assets, or did you stay the course? Understanding your responds to previous financial experiences can provide valuable insight. Additionally, consider life factors such as your age, income level, and financial obligations. Generally, younger investors with fewer responsibilities can afford to take more significant risks compared to someone nearing retirement. Balancing these aspects will help you arrive at a more precise assessment of your risk tolerance, enabling you to make informed decisions.

After determining your risk tolerance, the next step is to align your investment strategy accordingly. If you lean towards a higher risk tolerance, consider diversifying your portfolio with growth-oriented assets such as stocks or real estate investment trusts (REITs). These can provide higher returns over the long term, although they may also introduce more volatility. Conversely, if you identify yourself as risk-averse, it may be wiser to focus on more stable, income-generating investments like bonds or dividend-paying stocks. Balancing your portfolio between these asset classes based on your risk assessment will help you achieve a comfortable level of risk while still working toward your financial goals.

7.3 Building a Diversified Portfolio

Diversification is a fundamental concept in investing that emphasizes the importance of spreading your investments across various assets. The goal is to mitigate risk, as not all investments will perform the same at any given time. When you place your money in different asset classes — like stocks, bonds, real estate, or commodities — you're not overly dependent on the performance of a single investment. This helps cushion against market volatility. When one asset does poorly, another might perform well, balancing your overall portfolio. For those focused on financial independence and early retirement, understanding how to diversify effectively can significantly impact your long-term success.

Creating a balanced portfolio involves more than just dividing your money into different categories. It requires thoughtful strategies to ensure that your investments align with your risk tolerance, time horizon, and financial goals. Consider factors like asset allocation, which is all about how much money you put into each category. A typical approach is to have a mix of stocks and bonds, where younger investors might favor stocks for growth, while those closer to retirement lean towards safer bonds. Regularly reviewing and adjusting your allocations is key to staying on track. Dollar-cost averaging can also play a vital role, enabling investors to purchase more shares when prices are low and fewer when prices are high, which can improve overall returns over time.

Additionally, incorporating alternative investments, like real estate or peer-to-peer lending, can enhance your portfolio's diversification. These assets often behave differently from traditional stock and bond markets, providing further risk reduction. Keep in mind, though, that while diversification can minimize risks, it does not eliminate them entirely. Always maintain an element of knowledge about your investments; understanding what you own and why can empower you to make better decisions. As you build your portfolio, remember that having a diversified asset mix is crucial for not only preserving wealth but also achieving significant growth on your path to financial independence.

8. Retirement Accounts Explored

8.1 Types of Retirement Accounts

Retirement accounts are essential tools for building a secure financial future. Understanding the differences between traditional IRAs, Roth IRAs, 401(k)s, and SEP IRAs can empower individuals on their journey towards financial independence. Traditional IRAs allow you to contribute pre-tax dollars, which means you can reduce your taxable income in the year you contribute. The trade-off is that taxes will be due when you withdraw funds during retirement, typically at a potentially lower tax rate. Roth IRAs, on the other hand, require contributions to be made with after-tax dollars, allowing for tax-free withdrawals in retirement. This means that if you expect your tax rate to be higher in retirement, a Roth IRA could be the better option. 401(k)s are employer-sponsored plans that allow employees to save for retirement directly from their paycheck, often with an employer match. This match is essentially free money and can significantly accelerate your retirement savings. If you're self-employed or a small business owner, SEP IRAs offer a flexible option to contribute larger amounts than traditional or Roth IRAs, facilitating higher contributions based on company earnings. Each type of account has its own contribution limits, tax implications, and investment options, making it crucial to evaluate which aligns best with your financial goals and retirement timeline.

Choosing the right retirement account involves several factors. First, consider your current tax situation and your expected tax rate in retirement. If you anticipate being in a higher tax bracket later, a Roth IRA might be advantageous, allowing you to pay taxes now and enjoy tax-free withdrawals later. On the other hand, if you need a tax break right now, a traditional IRA could serve you better. Think about the importance of employer contributions; if your employer offers a 401(k) match, it's usually wise to prioritize that account to take full advantage of the match before considering other retirement options. Also, accessibility to funds is another critical feature involved in your choice. Early withdrawals can incur penalties, so if you think you may need to dip into your retirement savings, ensure you understand how each account handles early withdrawals. Lastly, consider your investment preferences and the available options within each account. Some plans may provide a wider variety of investment choices than others, affecting your potential growth. A hands-on investor may prefer a self-directed option, while others may want a more hands-off approach. Regardless of the path you choose, regularly reviewing your retirement accounts and ensuring they're aligned with your evolving financial goals is critical. For those aiming for financial independence, consistently contributing to retirement accounts is an essential step towards achieving early retirement. Setting up automatic contributions can help maintain consistency without the temptation to spend that money elsewhere.

8.2 Tax Advantages of Retirement Accounts

Understanding the tax features of various retirement accounts can have a significant impact on your financial strategies. Traditional retirement accounts, like 401(k)s and IRAs, allow you to make contributions with pre-tax dollars. This means that the money you contribute can lower your taxable income for the year, providing an immediate tax break. The taxes on these contributions, as well as any growth they generate while invested, are deferred until you withdraw the funds, typically in retirement. This can lead to a significant accumulation of wealth over time, especially if you start early. On the other hand, Roth accounts provide a different tax advantage. Contributions are made with after-tax dollars, so while you won't reduce your taxable income today, qualified withdrawals in retirement are entirely tax-free. This can be especially beneficial if you anticipate being in a higher tax bracket later in life.

Knowing the long-term benefits of these tax advantages can be crucial in your retirement planning. For instance, by maximizing contributions to a tax-deferred account, you can potentially grow your investments more significantly due to compounding effects. The longer your money remains invested without being taxed, the greater your total accumulation will be. Moreover, understanding the difference between tax-deferred and tax-free withdrawals can help you strategically plan your retirement income to minimize your overall tax burden. If you're planning for early retirement, this knowledge is even more relevant, as you'll need to manage your withdrawals to stretch your savings and maintain your lifestyle. When you have a clear strategy that leverages these tax features, you can optimize your financial trajectory, aligning it with your goals of financial independence.

A practical tip is to regularly review and adjust your contributions to ensure you're taking full advantage of your retirement accounts. Consider using tax projections to evaluate whether a Traditional or Roth account better suits your overall financial picture, especially as your income fluctuates. Staying informed about changes to tax laws and contribution limits can also help you maximize your retirement savings and minimize tax liabilities, making a meaningful difference in your financial independence journey.

8.3 Strategies for Maximizing Contributions

Maximizing contributions to retirement accounts is a crucial strategy for anyone seeking to achieve financial independence and early retirement. Understanding the maximum contribution limits set by tax authorities is the first step. For example, in the United States, individuals can contribute a certain amount to 401(k) plans or IRAs each year. These limits can change annually, so it's essential to stay updated. If possible, strive to contribute the maximum allowed. One effective technique is to set up automatic contributions. By automating your savings, you make investing effortless and consistent. This means a predetermined amount is deducted from your paycheck before you even see it, making it easier to save without the temptation to spend. Another approach is to take advantage of your employer's payroll deduction options if they offer them. This often makes it easier to reach the contribution limits without altering your budget dramatically. In addition to this, consider making catch-up contributions if you're over 50 years old, allowing you to deposit extra funds into your retirement accounts to bolster your savings as you approach retirement.

Employer matches can significantly boost your retirement savings, yet many employees fail to take full advantage of this benefit. When your employer offers a matching contribution, they essentially provide free money to your retirement account. Typically, employers will match a percentage of your contributions, up to a specified limit. To leverage this, it's crucial to contribute at least enough to receive the full match. If possible, go beyond the minimum contribution to increase your savings rate further. Many companies use a tiered matching system, where the match increases with the percentage of your contribution. Understanding your firm's policy can help you maximize these benefits. Additionally, be mindful of the vesting schedule, which determines when the employer's contributions truly belong to you. Knowing these details allows you to make informed decisions about your contributions, especially if you plan to leave your job. Whether you're looking to reach financial independence sooner or simply prepare for a comfortable retirement, taking full advantage of employer matches can lead to substantial growth in your retirement accounts.

Adopting these strategies can greatly enhance your savings journey. An effective method to track your contributions and stay motivated is to create a clear visual of your financial goals. This can be as simple as a spreadsheet or a more sophisticated budgeting app that allows you to monitor your progress. Understanding how much you are contributing relative to your goals can serve as a powerful motivator. In addition, regularly reviewing your financial situation ensures that you are on track to meet your targets. Moreover, regularly reassessing your budget to identify areas where you can save additional funds for retirement will further strengthen your position. This proactive approach combined with maximizing your contributions to retirement accounts and leveraging employer matches can set a solid foundation for achieving the financial freedom you desire.

9. Passive Income Streams

9.1 What is Passive Income?

Passive income refers to earnings derived from a rental property, limited partnership, or other enterprises in which a person is not actively involved. This form of income stands in contrast to active income, which is money earned through direct effort, like a salary from a job. With active income, you trade your time for money, meaning you have to work hours to receive your paycheck. In contrast, passive income allows you to earn money with little day-to-day effort once the initial setup is complete, creating an opportunity for financial growth without the constant grind of traditional employment. Understanding the difference between these income types is crucial for anyone looking to achieve financial independence and potentially retire early.

Generating passive income comes with numerous benefits that can significantly impact one's financial health. For starters, it provides an additional revenue stream that can supplement your primary income. This financial cushion not only enhances your overall income but also boosts your ability to save and invest. Moreover, passive income often allows for more flexibility in your lifestyle. It can free up your time, giving you the opportunity to pursue other passions or even explore additional income-generating avenues. Many individuals who adopt a strategy for passive income often find themselves less stressed about financial obligations, as they can still earn money while focusing on other aspects of life. The possibility of income growth through avenues like real estate or dividend stocks can also lead to more substantial wealth over time, offering a path toward financial stability and freedom.

To succeed in creating a stable source of passive income, it's important to start small and have a clear plan. Consider exploring various avenues such as rental properties, dividend-paying stocks, or even creating digital products that can sell continuously. Each of these options requires some initial investment of time or money, but once established, they can yield ongoing returns without constant effort. The key is to assess what aligns with your interests and resources, so you can build a sustainable income source that contributes to your long-term financial goals.

9.2 Different Types of Passive Income

Passive income can come from various sources, each offering unique opportunities and benefits. One common source is rental income, where property owners earn money by leasing out residential or commercial spaces. This method can provide a steady cash flow, especially in high-demand areas. Alternatively, dividends from stocks can be another significant form of passive income. By investing in stocks that pay regular dividends, individuals can enjoy returns without having to sell their shares. Additionally, online businesses, such as affiliate marketing or e-commerce, have become increasingly popular. These ventures often require an initial investment of time and resources to set up, but once established, they can generate income with minimal ongoing effort. Other sources may include peer-to-peer lending or creating digital products, like e-books or online courses, which can continue to sell long after they are created.

When evaluating passive income options, it's essential to consider which streams best align with your lifestyle and long-term financial goals. Assessing your current situation is a vital step; think about your available resources, time commitments, and financial priorities. For example, if you prefer a hands-off approach and have some capital to invest, rental properties or dividend stocks may suit you well. On the other hand, if you're willing to invest time upfront and have a knack for digital marketing, an online business might be the path for you. Understanding your strengths and weaknesses can help you choose passive income streams that you are not just capable of managing, but also will enjoy. It's also wise to consider risk factors and market trends, as these elements can affect the sustainability of your income sources over time.

To maximize your chances of success, diversifying your income streams can be beneficial. Relying on one source can be risky, as various external factors, such as economic downturns or changes in consumer behavior, can impact that income. By exploring multiple avenues—such as combining rental properties, dividend income, and online business ventures—you can create a more resilient financial strategy. Remember, building passive income takes patience and persistence. Regularly reassess your income sources to ensure they continue to align with your goals and adjust as necessary. As you embark on this journey toward financial independence, remember that every small step you take contributes to your larger goal of achieving early retirement.

9.3 Building Your Passive Income Portfolio

Creating a passive income portfolio begins with the understanding that your first step is to assess your financial situation. Analyze your income, expenses, and savings to identify how much you can allocate towards building your passive income streams. Begin with setting clear goals, whether it's saving a specific amount for retirement or generating enough income to cover your lifestyle. Research different streams such as real estate investments, dividend stocks, peer-to-peer lending, or creating digital products. Each of these options requires varying levels of initial investment and ongoing effort. Choose what fits best with your risk tolerance and interests. Start small by perhaps investing in a dividend-paying stock or a real estate investment trust (REIT). The key is to stay consistent and reinvest the returns back into your portfolio to compound your wealth over time.

Scaling your income is the next step once you have established your portfolio. Look for ways to increase your earnings from the initial passive income sources you have developed. For instance, if you have invested in rental property, consider renovations that will allow you to increase the rent or explore short-term rental platforms for higher returns. In the realm of stocks, reinvest dividends to purchase more shares, growing the income generated. Diversifying your income streams is also crucial; instead of relying on one source, expand by incorporating multiple forms of passive income. This could mean branching out into different sectors or asset types. Besides, keep an eye on emerging opportunities and stay adaptable as market conditions change. Consider automating your investments to maintain discipline and ensure your portfolio continues to grow, freeing you to focus on other aspects of life.

As you embark on your journey of building and scaling your passive income portfolio, remember that patience and persistence are essential. It may take time for your income to grow, but the reward is worth the effort. A practical tip to keep in mind is to regularly review your portfolio. Set a schedule, perhaps quarterly, to assess the performance of your investments and make adjustments as needed. This will help you stay aligned with your financial goals and ensure that your journey towards financial independence is on the right track.

10. The Role of Insurance

10.1 Insurance Types You Need

Understanding the basics of insurance is vital for achieving financial security. Different types of insurance can protect your assets, health, and income, safeguarding your financial future. First and foremost is health insurance, which covers medical expenses, ensuring that a significant health event doesn't drain your savings. Then, there's life insurance, especially important if you have dependents. This policy provides financial support for your loved ones after you're gone, helping them maintain their standard of living. Homeowners or renters insurance protects your property against damage or theft and is crucial if you want to safeguard your belongings. Furthermore, auto insurance isn't just a legal requirement in many places; it protects you from financial loss in case of accidents or theft of your vehicle. Each of these insurance types plays a crucial role in your financial strategy, creating a safety net that helps you manage life's uncertainties.

Selecting the right insurance policies requires careful consideration of your personal circumstances and needs. Begin by assessing your current situation, including your income, assets, and health status. This self-assessment will guide you in determining the level of coverage you require. It's also essential to shop around for quotes from multiple insurers. Different companies can offer varying rates for similar coverage. Take the time to read the fine print to understand what is covered and any exclusions that may apply. Additionally, consider the reputation of the insurance provider by checking customer reviews and financial stability ratings. It's not just about the price; you also want a reliable company that will be there when you need them. Finding the right balance between cost and coverage is key to securing your financial independence.

As you explore insurance options, remember that it's not a one-time decision. Your needs may change over time, requiring you to adjust your coverage. Regularly reviewing your policies ensures that they still align with your financial goals and personal situation. Additionally, consider bundling multiple insurance types, like home and auto, for potential discounts. The peace of mind provided by adequate insurance is invaluable as you work towards FIRE. Keep in mind that investing in proper insurance can save you from significant financial setbacks in the future, allowing you to focus on your path to financial independence.

10.2 *Evaluating Your Insurance Needs*

Understanding your insurance needs is crucial, especially as you navigate through different stages of life. Each phase brings unique risks, requiring a tailored approach to insurance. Start by evaluating your current situation: consider your age, family structure, health status, and financial responsibilities. For example, young adults or newlyweds may primarily need health and liability coverage, while those with children might focus on life insurance and educational savings plans. As your responsibilities grow, so do your insurance needs. Reflect on potential risks; think about the impact on your loved ones if you were unable to work or if a significant event occurred. It's also important to check if your career or hobbies expose you to additional risks that need coverage.

Utilizing methods such as risk assessment questionnaires can help clarify your insurance needs. These tools can guide you through evaluating the likelihood and impact of different risks in your life. Furthermore, consider consulting with a financial advisor who specializes in insurance. They can provide insights tailored to your situation and help you create a comprehensive insurance strategy that aligns with your financial goals, especially if you're pursuing financial independence or early retirement.

Once you understand your insurance needs, it's vital to review your current policies to identify any gaps in coverage. Many people unknowingly rely on inadequate policies or miss critical insurance products. Start by taking stock of what you have: review your life, health, home, and auto insurance policies. Look closely for exclusions or limits in coverage that might leave you vulnerable in case of a loss. For instance, are you adequately covered for natural disasters? Does your homeowner's policy include valuable possessions like jewelry or collectibles?

Addressing these gaps could involve increasing policy limits, adding riders, or even exploring new types of insurance such as umbrella policies that provide additional liability protection. Remember, your insurance needs can shift significantly as your financial situation changes. Conduct regular reviews, especially after life events like marriage, the birth of a child, or a new job. Staying proactive about your insurance will not only safeguard your financial independence journey, but also ensure that your loved ones are protected from unforeseen circumstances.

One practical tip is to set a calendar reminder to review your insurance policies annually. This simple act can help you prevent coverage lapses and ensure your insurance aligns with your ever-evolving life and financial goals.

10.3 Minimizing Your Insurance Costs

Cost-reduction strategies are crucial for anyone aiming for financial independence, particularly when it comes to managing insurance premiums. One effective approach is to increase your deductible. By doing this, you agree to pay more out-of-pocket in the event of a claim, but it significantly reduces your premium cost. Another method is to bundle insurance policies, such as combining home and auto insurance with the same provider. Many companies offer discounts for bundling, which can lead to substantial savings. Additionally, regularly reviewing your coverage limits can help ensure you're not over-insured. While it's essential to have sufficient coverage, adjusting limits based on your current needs or life changes can help lower costs. You should also inquire about discounts for various reasons, including being a member of specific organizations, maintaining a good driving record, or even having a home security system in place. This proactive approach can often reveal savings that might not be immediately apparent.

Shopping for insurance is another vital aspect of minimizing costs. The importance of comparing policies and providers cannot be overstated. Every insurance company has different pricing structures, and rates can vary significantly for the same coverage. Start by gathering quotes from multiple providers, making sure to assess the same parameters for each so you're comparing apples to apples. Look for online tools that make this process easier, allowing you to input your information once and receive multiple quotes. It's also helpful to read customer reviews and consider the reputation of each company, as service quality can vary widely. Furthermore, consider working with an independent insurance agent who can help you navigate the maze of options and find the best deals tailored to your specific needs.

In the quest for minimizing insurance costs, consistently reviewing and adjusting your insurance policies as your life circumstances change can save you a good amount of money. Make it a routine to look over your insurance every year, and don't hesitate to switch providers if you find better coverage at a lower price. This diligence not only helps keep your costs down but also ensures that you're always getting the best value for your insurance. Be proactive in your search for savings, as even minor adjustments can accumulate to significant financial benefits, moving you closer to your financial independence and early retirement goals.

11. Tax Planning for FIRE

11.1 *Understanding Your Tax Bracket*

Understanding tax brackets is essential for anyone looking to manage their money effectively. Tax brackets are essentially ranges of income that are taxed at specific rates. This means that as your income increases, the additional income is taxed at higher rates, but only the amount exceeding a threshold falls into the higher bracket. For example, if you earn $50,000 and the tax bracket for that income is 12%, you will pay 12% on every dollar earned within that range, but if your income increases to $70,000, only the portion exceeding $50,000 would be taxed at whichever rate applies to that higher bracket, not the entire income. This system is designed to ensure that people with higher incomes contribute a fairer share in taxes, while still providing relief to those earning less.

Your income level significantly shapes your tax responsibilities, and understanding this impact can help you make informed financial decisions. If you're making strides towards financial independence or early retirement, the taxes you pay now can affect how quickly you reach your goals. For example, realizing income in the higher tax brackets can increase your tax liability where you may pay more than if you strategically plan your taxable income over several years. Many individuals in the Financial Independence and Early Retirement (FIRE) community look for ways to minimize their tax burden, whether through tax-advantaged accounts, deductions, or tax-efficient investing strategies. This often includes keeping your annual income within specific thresholds to stay in lower brackets, thereby allowing your investments to grow while minimizing taxes. It's important to regularly assess your financial situation and consider how fluctuations in income can influence your overall financial strategy. By being aware of how tax brackets work, you can better strategize your earnings to enhance your financial health and progress toward your FIRE aspirations.

11.2 Tax-efficient Investment Strategies

Investing wisely is more than just picking the right stocks or assets; it also involves strategic planning to minimize tax liabilities. Understanding the tax implications of your investment choices can significantly impact your overall returns. One effective approach is to hold investments long-term. Generally, long-term capital gains—the profit from selling assets held for more than a year—are taxed at a lower rate than short-term gains. This can lead to substantial tax savings. Consider exploring tax-loss harvesting as well. This strategy involves selling investments that have declined in value to offset taxes on gains from other investments. By carefully managing your portfolio in this way, you can effectively reduce your overall tax burden. Additionally, being mindful of the types of investments you hold in different accounts is crucial. For example, interest from bonds is typically taxed as ordinary income, while qualified dividends and capital gains are often taxed at a lower rate. Placing less tax-efficient assets in tax-deferred accounts can help preserve more of your returns.

Utilizing tax-sheltered accounts is another cornerstone of an effective tax-efficient investment strategy. Accounts like a 401(k), Traditional IRA, or Roth IRA offer significant tax advantages that can accelerate wealth building. With a 401(k) or Traditional IRA, contributions are usually made pre-tax, reducing your taxable income for the year and allowing your investments to grow tax-deferred until withdrawal. This means you can reinvest earnings without immediate tax implications. On the other hand, Roth IRAs lend the advantage of tax-free growth and withdrawals, provided certain conditions are met. Another option is Health Savings Accounts (HSAs), which can be a triple tax advantage; contributions are tax deductible, grow tax-free, and withdrawals for qualified medical spends are also tax-free. Maximizing contributions to these accounts can enhance your investment returns by minimizing the taxes you owe. These strategies not only boost your current savings but also set you up for financial independence by allowing your investments to compound over time.

One practical tip to optimize your tax strategies is to regularly review your portfolio for tax efficiency. This includes assessing which assets are held where and considering any potential tax implications of selling or reallocating investments. Timing can be critical; for example, if you anticipate being in a lower tax bracket in the future, it might make sense to defer selling appreciated assets until then. Staying informed about changing tax laws and considering consulting a tax professional can also provide guidance tailored to your financial situation, ensuring you make the most of your investment strategies while adhering to tax regulations.

11.3 Deductions and Credits to Consider

Understanding common deductions is essential to reducing your taxable income. These deductions can include business expenses, student loan interest, contributions to retirement accounts, and even certain medical expenses. For instance, if you are self-employed, you may deduct costs incurred for your business, such as home office expenses, supplies, and travel related to your job. Additionally, if you've taken out student loans, you can often deduct a portion of the interest paid each year. It's worth exploring whether you qualify for the standard deduction or itemized deductions, as this can significantly affect your taxable income. Each taxpayer's situation is unique, so it's wise to familiarize yourself with the specific deductions available to you and to keep solid records throughout the year to maximize your potential savings.

Maximizing tax credits can be just as powerful as taking deductions, if not more so, because credits directly reduce the amount of tax you owe. Exploring available tax credits can offer significant financial benefits. Some popular credits include the Earned Income Tax Credit, which supports low to moderate-income workers, and the Child Tax Credit, which provides relief for those with dependent children. Many taxpayers overlook education credits such as the American Opportunity Credit or the Lifetime Learning Credit, which can help offset the cost of higher education. Actively seeking out and claiming these credits can substantially improve your overall tax outcome. It's important to stay up-to-date with tax legislation since new credits may become available, and existing ones could change from year to year.

Incorporating deductions and credits into your tax strategy requires diligence and awareness, but doing so can lead to substantial savings. Keeping organized records, learning about your eligibility for various deductions and credits, and consulting with a tax professional when necessary are all steps you can take to enhance your personal finance and budgeting strategies. As a practical tip, make it a habit to review your tax situation mid-year, so you can plan accordingly and ensure you're making the most of the deductions and credits available to you.

12. Lifestyle Design

12.1 Aligning Lifestyle with Values

Identifying personal values is an essential first step in shaping your financial decisions. Start by reflecting on what truly matters to you. Consider aspects like family, health, experiences, security, creativity, and community. Write down the five to ten core values that resonate with you the most. Once you have this list, think critically about how these values influence your lifestyle and financial choices. For instance, if one of your top values is health, you might prioritize spending on healthy food, gym memberships, or fitness classes. Likewise, if family is paramount, you may allocate more resources toward family vacations or quality time spent together. This values assessment not only guides your spending decisions but also helps you trim unnecessary expenses that do not align with what you care about most.

Integrating your values into daily spending requires intentionality. Start by scrutinizing your current expenditures; categorize them in relation to your core values. It's helpful to create a spending plan that includes value-driven categories. For example, if creativity is a significant value, ensure there is a line item in your budget for classes, materials, or experiences that foster that aspect of your life. This approach is about consciously choosing where your money goes rather than letting it slip away on things that don't bring value. Consider using budgeting tools to visualize your spending against your values. By assessing your purchases regularly, you can adjust accordingly, ensuring that every dollar spent aligns with your principles.

To maintain alignment over time, revisiting your values periodically is beneficial. Life changes, and so do priorities. Set aside time every few months to reflect on whether your spending still aligns with your values. Engaging in this practice creates ongoing awareness of financial choices and reinforces the commitment to a life congruent with what you hold dear. A practical tip for this process is to have a "values check-in" every time you make a significant purchase. Ask yourself how this purchase brings you closer to living out your values. This simple question can help you make more mindful financial choices that support your journey toward financial independence and early retirement.

12.2 Minimalism and Its Financial Benefits

Understanding minimalism goes beyond just having fewer possessions. It's about a mindset that prioritizes value over volume, simplicity over excess, and purpose over distraction. When applied to finance, minimalism emphasizes the significance of intentional spending and mindful decision-making. This philosophy encourages individuals to reflect on their true needs and desires, distancing themselves from societal pressures to consume. By identifying what truly matters, individuals can align their financial choices with their long-term goals, making it easier to pursue financial independence and early retirement.

Adopting minimalism can be a powerful strategy for reducing expenses and accumulating wealth. As you simplify your life, you'll likely find that many expenses can be eliminated or reduced. For example, by minimizing clutter and distractions, you may begin to notice how much you spend on non-essential items. This realization often leads to cutting back on impulse purchases, streaming services, or even expensive memberships that don't provide genuine value. As you embrace a minimalist lifestyle, you'll start to see tangible financial benefits, freeing up resources that can be redirected toward savings or investments.

Incorporating minimalism into your financial habits is not just about saving money; it's also about creating an environment conducive to achieving your financial aspirations. Consider tracking your spending to identify areas where you can cut back, focusing on quality instead of quantity. Investing in experiences rather than possessions can also yield greater satisfaction and personal fulfillment. Practicing minimalism can ultimately help you forge a clearer path toward financial independence, showing that less can truly be more. When considering small changes, starting with a budget review and setting clear financial goals can empower you to take meaningful steps toward a minimalist approach to your finances.

12.3 Creating a Vision Board for Your Future

Visualizing your goals is a powerful tool when it comes to achieving your financial dreams. A vision board serves as a tangible representation of what you aspire to become, helping to clarify and prioritize your financial objectives. By incorporating images, quotes, and symbols that resonate with your dreams of financial independence and early retirement, you create a visual reminder of your aspirations. This process not only helps in identifying your goals but also strengthens your commitment to achieving them. When you look at your vision board, you reinforce your desire to improve your financial situation, making it easier to visualize the steps you need to take to get there.

Staying focused on your FIRE journey can be challenging, especially with distractions around you. Your vision board can be an invaluable motivational tool during tough times. Place it in a visible spot in your home or workspace so that you see it regularly. This consistent exposure keeps your financial goals at the forefront of your mind, reminding you why you are pursuing financial independence. Consider updating your board periodically to reflect any changes in your goals or progress, which can help maintain your enthusiasm and drive. Engaging with your vision board daily through visualization exercises, such as taking a few moments to imagine living the life you desire, can enhance your motivation and commitment to achieving your financial freedom.

A practical tip for using your vision board effectively is to set specific, measurable targets alongside your images and words. Instead of simply including a picture of a dream home, specify the amount needed for a down payment or the yearly savings goal to reach that milestone. This approach not only makes your goals more concrete but also allows you to track progress in a more focused way. Allow your vision board to serve as a dynamic part of your financial journey, helping you to visualize success while actively working towards it.

13. Overcoming Psychological Barriers

13.1 The Emotional Impact of Money

Emotional relationships with money can be complex and deeply rooted in our upbringing, experiences, and societal influences. Understanding how feelings toward money shape our financial decisions is crucial. For many, money represents security, freedom, and self-worth. Others may associate it with stress, anxiety, or feelings of inadequacy. These emotional ties can significantly affect not just how we manage money, but also how we perceive our financial situations and the choices we make about spending, saving, and investing. When financial stress becomes overwhelming, it hampers our ability to focus on long-term goals, often leading to impulsive decisions or avoidance altogether. Cultivating a positive emotional relationship with money involves recognizing these feelings without judgment, enabling a healthier and more constructive approach to finances.

Recognizing patterns in money beliefs is a transformative step toward financial independence. Many of us carry subconscious beliefs that stem from our childhood or cultural backgrounds, such as "money is the root of all evil" or "I will never be good with money." These harmful beliefs can create mental barriers that hinder financial growth and stability. Identifying these ingrained thoughts is essential; it allows you to confront and challenge them. Journaling your beliefs about money, discussing them with a trusted friend, or engaging in financial coaching can help bring these patterns to light. Once you've acknowledged these toxic beliefs, you can replace them with more positive and empowering narratives, enhancing your ability to manage your finances effectively and reach your goals.

To foster a healthy relationship with money, consider implementing practices that promote mindfulness and gratitude in your financial dealings. Regularly reflecting on the positive aspects of your financial situation, no matter how small, can shift your focus from scarcity to abundance. This outlook not only reduces anxiety but also encourages wise financial behaviors. As you practice gratitude, you might find it easier to set meaningful financial goals aligned with your values, steering your journey toward financial independence and early retirement with clarity and purpose.

13.2 Cultivating a Wealth Mindset

Positive thinking is a powerful tool for developing a mindset that attracts financial success. Visualizing your financial goals is one of the most effective techniques to strengthen this mindset. When you can see what your success looks like—whether that's a fully funded retirement account or a debt-free life—you can begin to work toward those goals with intention. Surrounding yourself with affirmations related to wealth can also help. Phrases such as I am capable of achieving financial freedom can rewire your brain to focus on abundance rather than scarcity. Additionally, seeking out stories of others who have achieved financial independence can inspire you and provide a roadmap for your journey. Consider keeping a journal where you reflect on your financial victories, no matter how small. This practice not only boosts your confidence but also reinforces a success-oriented mindset.

Reframing setbacks is crucial for anyone on the path to financial independence. Instead of viewing financial challenges as insurmountable obstacles, recognize them as valuable learning opportunities. When faced with unexpected expenses, think about what lessons you can extract from the experience. For example, if a car repair sets you back financially, consider how this can encourage you to build or enhance your emergency fund. Understanding that financial challenges are often a part of the journey can reduce stress and promote resilience. Embracing a mindset that appreciates growth through difficulty can empower you to take decisive action. By acknowledging setbacks as integral to your personal financial education, you transform the narrative from anxiety to growth, making each hurdle a stepping stone toward your financial goals.

Developing a wealth mindset also involves practicing gratitude for what you currently have. Regularly acknowledging your resources, skills, and the support systems around you shifts your perspective from lack to abundance. This simple act can create a positive feedback loop that keeps you motivated and focused on achieving your financial dreams. Remember, cultivating a wealth mindset is a journey, not a destination. Small, consistent changes in how you think about money can propel you toward financial independence and ultimately allow you to enjoy life on your terms.

13.3 Staying Motivated on Your FIRE Journey

Setting milestones is crucial in any long-term journey, especially when aiming for financial independence. Celebrating small wins provides a sense of accomplishment that fuels your motivation. Each step you take, whether it's saving a certain amount, paying off a debt, or reaching a savings goal, deserves to be acknowledged. These small victories create a momentum that keeps you engaged in your overall mission. For instance, if you manage to reduce your monthly expenses by a certain percentage, take a moment to reward yourself, perhaps by enjoying a simple treat or taking a day off to relax. This recognition of progress helps to reframe the often overwhelming nature of the journey into manageable and rewarding parts. Instead of feeling like you are waiting indefinitely for that big financial goal to be achieved, you create a pattern of success that reinforces your commitment and enhances your enjoyment along the way.

Community support plays an equally important role in maintaining motivation on your path to FIRE. Connecting with like-minded individuals who share similar goals can be incredibly uplifting. Sharing your experiences, challenges, and successes within a community fosters a sense of belonging that combats feelings of isolation. Whether through online forums, social media groups, or local meetups, these networks provide encouragement and accountability. Hearing stories from others who are also on this journey can inspire you to keep pushing forward, especially during tough times. They can offer practical tips, share valuable resources, and remind you that you are not alone in the pursuit of financial freedom. Engaging with a supportive community strengthens your resolve and reinforces your commitment to your goals, making the entire process feel more achievable and enjoyable.

Remember that motivation can fluctuate, and that's perfectly normal. The key is to create a sustainable pathway that incorporates celebrating your progress and engaging with a supportive network. By continually acknowledging your small achievements and seeking out encouragement from others, you build a resilient mindset that can withstand the ups and downs of your FIRE journey. A practical tip is to set aside a little time each week to reflect on your progress and reach out to at least one person in your support network. This simple practice can rejuvenate your spirit and keep you on track towards your financial goals.

14. Creating a Support System

14.1 Building a Community of Like-minded Individuals

Networking is a powerful tool that can significantly enhance your journey toward financial independence and early retirement. Connecting with others who share similar financial goals can provide a wealth of advantages. When you surround yourself with people who think like you, you not only gain supportive friends but also access invaluable insights and resources. Discussing budgeting strategies, investment opportunities, and saving techniques can help you refine your own methods and stay motivated. Sharing your experiences and challenges with others allows for mutual learning, where everyone benefits from each other's successes and setbacks. The conversations that spark in these networks often unveil new strategies for achieving financial milestones, making the road to your goals feel less isolating and more attainable.

Finding the right communities is crucial to building this supportive network. You can start by identifying both online and local groups that resonate with your aspirations. Online platforms like forums, social media groups, and specialized websites host myriad communities devoted to FIRE principles. Additionally, local meetups and workshops create a tangible space to engage with others who are just as passionate about financial freedom. Look for events in your area by checking community boards, libraries, or even local cafes that may hold financial seminars. Once you find a group, don't hesitate to dive in. Participate actively, share your own stories, and ask questions. The more you engage, the more you'll benefit from the collective experiences and advice of your peers.

Creating connections with like-minded individuals can transform your approach to personal finance. Not only does it offer accountability, but it also fosters a sense of belonging and encouragement. As you gather knowledge from your network, consider sharing your insights as well. Teaching others can deepen your own understanding and reinforce your commitment to your financial goals. Also, attending or organizing regular meetups can shift the focus from individual struggles to collective success. Remember that building a community is an ongoing process, and every interaction is a step toward securing your financial future.

14.2 Utilizing Online Resources

In today's digital age, navigating through the vast landscape of online resources can feel overwhelming. However, there are numerous valuable financial tools and websites that can support your journey toward financial independence and early retirement. Start by exploring budgeting apps like Mint and YNAB, which help you track your spending and create personalized budgets. These platforms not only let you see where your money goes but can also integrate with your bank accounts for easy management. Furthermore, websites like Personal Capital offer robust financial planning and investment tracking tools that give you a clear picture of your net worth and progress toward your financial goals. Additionally, don't underestimate the power of spreadsheets. Templates available on Google Sheets or Excel can be customized for budgeting, tracking debts, or calculating how long it will take to reach your FIRE target, offering a straightforward way to monitor your finances.

Engaging with the personal finance community through blogs, podcasts, and online forums can significantly enrich your understanding of various financial strategies. Many personal finance bloggers share their journeys toward financial independence, offering firsthand insights that can inspire and educate you. Websites like Mr. Money Mustache and The Financial Samurai are excellent starting points, full of practical tips and life lessons learned along the way. Podcasts like The Mad Fientist Podcast and ChooseFI delve into detailed interviews with experts and everyday people who have successfully navigated the path to FIRE, providing relatable stories and actionable advice. Forums such as Reddit's r/financialindependence are vibrant spaces where you can ask questions, share experiences, and get feedback from others who are on the same journey. Being part of these communities can motivate you and equip you with the tools and knowledge necessary to take control of your financial destiny.

For those looking to dive deeper, consider setting aside time each week to explore these resources. Bookmark your favorite blogs, subscribe to a couple of podcasts that resonate with you, and participate in discussions online. This way, you'll continuously feed your mind with new ideas and strategies that can propel you toward your financial goals.

14.3 Finding a Financial Mentor

Identifying the right mentor can significantly influence your financial journey. Start by looking for individuals who have achieved what you're aspiring to, whether it's financial independence, successful investment strategies, or a savvy approach to budgeting. Attend local financial workshops, seminars, and networking events where you can meet potential mentors. Online platforms like LinkedIn can also help you connect with professionals in your field of interest. When you find someone whose achievements resonate with you, don't hesitate to reach out. Introduce yourself and express your admiration for their work, and ask if they would be open to sharing their insights. Approach potential mentors with specific questions or topics in mind, which will show that you're serious about your financial growth. Remember, mentors are often busy, so be respectful of their time and show genuine interest in their experiences.

Building a mentor-mentee relationship is crucial for gaining the most from this experience. Once you establish contact with a mentor, keep the lines of communication open. Regular check-ins, whether through emails or casual coffee chats, can strengthen your connection. Always come prepared with questions, updates on your financial decisions, and what you've learned since your last conversation. Show appreciation for their guidance and consider reciprocating in ways that demonstrate your gratitude, whether through a simple thank you or sharing relevant information that aligns with their interests. Nurturing this relationship paves the way for a fruitful exchange. Remember, mentorship is a two-way street; your mentor may also appreciate insights or assistance you can offer in return.

A practical tip to enhance your mentoring experience is to document your journey. Keep a journal of your discussions, insights, and any actionable steps you take based on your mentor's advice. Not only does this create a record of your growth, but it also serves as a reminder of progress when you face challenges. Reflect periodically on the lessons learned and how they apply to your financial goals. This practice not only helps solidify your learning but also shows your mentor that you value their input and are committed to your financial independence journey.

15. Transitioning to Early Retirement

15.1 Preparing for the Shift

Mindset change is one of the most crucial aspects of preparing for retirement. Transitioning from the structured environment of work to the freedom of retirement can feel daunting. Many people find their identities are deeply tied to their careers, making it essential to redefine who you are outside of that role. It's helpful to start shifting your mindset by embracing the idea that retirement is not an end, but rather the beginning of a new chapter filled with possibilities. Engage in self-reflection to uncover interests or hobbies you've sidelined during your working years. This preparation involves not only envisioning how you will spend your newfound time but also addressing any fears associated with the change. Consider thinking about what your daily life will look like after leaving work and actively seeking ways to create a fulfilling routine that excites you.

Transitioning into retirement also requires practical steps to ensure a smooth logistical shift. Begin by organizing your finances well in advance. Calculate your expected income sources, such as pensions, social security, and investment returns as they will need careful management. Creating a detailed budget that outlines your anticipated expenses is critical. This should include potential healthcare costs, leisure activities, and any other expenses unique to your lifestyle. It's also wise to assess any outstanding debts, as eliminating these before retirement can lead to a more comfortable journey. Furthermore, consider how you will manage your assets; this might mean reassessing your investment strategy or consulting with a financial advisor to ensure your retirement savings are secure.

By the time you approach your retirement date, all these elements come together to form a solid foundation for this new phase of life. It's beneficial to have a contingency plan for unexpected expenses or changes in your health. Regularly reviewing your plans and financial status ensures you remain on track and can make adjustments as needed. One practical tip is to simulate a typical retirement week before officially leaving work. Try filling your schedule with activities you envision doing after retirement. This exercise can provide insights into whether you're adequately prepared both mentally and financially for the lifestyle you aim to adopt.

15.2 Managing Your Time After Retirement

Time management after retirement is crucial for a fulfilling life. While you may have said goodbye to the 9-to-5 grind, structuring your days can help you maintain a sense of purpose and productivity. Start by setting a daily routine. Following the same daily structure can provide a framework that brings balance to your newfound freedom. Consider scheduling blocks of time for tasks you want to accomplish, whether they are chores, personal projects, or simply enjoying a good book in your favorite chair. Utilize calendars or digital planners to keep track of appointments and activities, making it easier to allocate time for everything you value.

Additionally, prioritize your tasks using the Eisenhower Box or similar strategies to help determine what is urgent and important. This technique can assist you in focusing on what matters most, ensuring that you dedicate time to pursuits that genuinely enhance your life. More importantly, remember to leave room for spontaneity. Retirement gives you the freedom to be flexible, allowing those unexpected moments of joy to enrich your days.

Retirement is the perfect opportunity to delve into hobbies and interests that you always wanted to pursue but never had the time for. Whether it's painting, gardening, or learning a new language, engaging in these activities can greatly enhance your quality of life. Investing your time into hobbies not only brings personal satisfaction but also offers a chance to connect with like-minded individuals, thereby building a social network that adds joy to your days. Consider joining local clubs, attending workshops, or even participating in online courses that allow you to explore your passions. Remember that the goal is not just to fill your time but to cultivate joy and fulfillment in your everyday life.

Lastly, it's essential to integrate healthy habits into your new routine. Exercise, whether through walking, biking, or yoga, can be incredibly beneficial for both physical and mental well-being. Finding ways to stay active will enrich your retirement experience and help maintain your financial independence by potentially lowering healthcare costs in the long run. As you explore this new chapter in your life, a practical takeaway is to keep your mindset open and adaptable. Embrace flexibility, and adjust your plans as you discover new interests and activities that inspire and excite you.

15.3 Staying Financially Fit in Retirement

Budgeting in retirement requires a shift in mindset and approach. Unlike in your working years, where income flows regularly from a paycheck, retirement often means relying on a fixed income that can come from various sources like Social Security, pensions, and savings. Understanding how to manage these funds effectively is crucial to ensuring that your money lasts as long as you do.

Start by taking a close look at your expected income sources and expenses. Create a comprehensive list of your monthly expenditures, which should include essentials like housing, healthcare, groceries, and transportation, as well as discretionary spending. It's common for some expenses to decrease, such as commuting costs, while others, particularly healthcare, may rise as you age. By understanding your complete financial picture, you can identify areas where you may need to adjust your spending. You should also consider utilizing budgeting tools and apps to keep everything organized. These resources can help you track your spending in real-time, enabling you to make adjustments swiftly if necessary.

As your financial situation evolves, it's important to revisit your budget regularly. An annual review can help you adjust for any changes in income or expenses, ensuring that your financial plan remains aligned with your goals. Automation can also be beneficial; setting up automatic transfers for bills or savings can streamline your financial management and reduce the risk of late payments. Building a small cushion in your budget for unexpected expenses can alleviate stress and make your financial situation feel more secure. Remember, flexibility is key. Allow your budget to adapt as your needs and circumstances change over time.

Retirement is not the end of your financial education; it should be viewed as a new chapter that invites continual learning and adaptation. The financial landscape is constantly changing, from new investment opportunities to tax laws that can affect your retirement savings and withdrawals. Staying informed about these changes can empower you to make better financial decisions.

Consider attending workshops, enrolling in online courses, or reading financial books tailored to retirement strategies. Engaging with personal finance blogs, podcasts, or forums can provide insights and diverse perspectives that keep you informed about best practices and emerging trends in financial management. Connecting with professionals like financial advisors can also be invaluable, as they can offer personalized advice and strategies suited to your unique situation.

Participating in discussion groups or communities focused on financial independence and early retirement can foster a supportive environment where you can share experiences and learn from others. This ongoing education not only enhances your financial knowledge but also gives you the confidence to adapt your plan as needed throughout retirement. Staying proactive about your financial education will help you navigate any changes effectively and position you favorably to pursue your goals.

A practical tip is to set aside a small portion of your time each month to enhance your financial literacy. Whether it's reading an article, listening to a financial podcast, or attending a seminar, this commitment can make a significant difference over the long term.

www.ingramcontent.com/pod-product-compliance
Lightning Source LLC
Chambersburg PA
CBHW070213230526
45471CB00002B/941